21ST CENTURY DEBATES

GLOBAL DEBT

THE IMPACT ON OUR LIVES

TERESA GARLAKE

RAINTREE STECK-VAUGHN PUBLISHERS

A Harcourt Company

Austin   New York

www.raintreesteckvaughn.com

21st Century Debates Series

Genetics • Surveillance • Internet • Media • Artificial Intelligence • Climate Change • Energy • Rain Forests • Waste, Recycling, and Reuse • Endangered Species • Air Pollution • An Overcrowded World? • Food Supply • Water Supply • World Health • Drugs • Terrorism • Racism • New Religious Movements • Violence in Society • Tourism • Transportation and the Environment

Copyright Permissions
Steck-Vaughn Company
P.O. Box 26015
Austin, TX 78755

Published by Raintree Steck-Vaughn Publishers, an imprint of Steck-Vaughn Company

Library of Congress Cataloging-in-Publication Data

Cataloging-in-publication data is available at the Library of Congress

ISBN 0-7398-6035-6

Printed in Hong Kong by Wing King Tong Co. Ltd.
1 2 3 4 5 6 7 8 9 LB 07 06 05 04 03

Picture credits: Andes Press Agency 52 (Carlos Reyes-Manzo); Camera Press 56 (J. Charles Chatard); HWPL 5 (Julia Waterlow), 10 and 58 (David Cumming), 20, 26, 33, 46, 50; Panos Pictures 4 (Susan Hackett), 7 (Stefan Boness), 8 (Trygve Bolstad), 21 (Betty Press), 39 (Giacomo Pirozzi); Popperfoto 14, 36 (Fabrizio Bensch), 37, 40 (United Press-Acme Photo), 43 (Kimimasa Mayama), 44 (Yuri Cortez), 45 (Rafiqur Rahman), 49; South American Pictures 13 (Tony Morrison); Still Pictures 6, 17, 19, 27 and 59 (Ron Giling), 22 (Toby Adamson), 23 and 29 (Jorgen Schytte), 24, 25 (Hartmut Schwarzbach), 28 (Hjalte Tin), 30, 32 and 42 (Mark Edwards), 34 (Paul Glendell), 35 (S. Cytrynowicz-Christian Aid), 55 (Adrian Arbib); Topham/The Image Works 53; WTPix (Chris Fairclough) 18 , cover foreground, cover background.

Acknowledgements
The case studies of individuals mentioned in this book have been gathered from a range of sources: Alfredo and Lucy: *Forever in Your Debt*, Christian Aid, 1998; the Radley family (not their real name): Church Action on Poverty; Kishnan: *Indian Express* Newspapers; Julio Cespedes: *Who Runs the World?*, Christian Aid, 1994; Angelus Mtego, the *Guardian* newspaper; Emma Tshamputu, *No Excuses: Facing up to sub-Saharan Africa's AIDS orphans crisis*, Christian Aid, 2001; Lefkata Jere/Jovana Cruz Condor, *New Internationalist* magazine.

Cover: foreground picture shows a young Kenyan girl carrying a baby in a sling on her back; background picture shows high-rise buildings in Hong Kong.

CONTENTS

WHAT IS DEBT?

Alfredo's class is overcrowded. There are not enough desks and the roof leaks. He goes to school in the evenings. Although he is only fourteen years old, he works during the day. This is because education in Bolivia is no longer free. Like many of his classmates, Alfredo's parents cannot afford to pay for school and so he pays his own way. Halfway across the world, Lucy is a health worker in Mavala village in Tanzania. She used to receive a government salary for her work but she has not been paid for many months now. The villagers help out by paying her what they can. But they too are getting poorer and it is getting harder to spare any money.

Alfredo and Lucy will never meet but they have much in common. Their governments are caught in a debt trap. Repaying loans to international lenders means that governments cannot spend money on the education and health of their citizens. Alfredo and Lucy are just two victims of a debt crisis that affects the lives and dreams of countless people living in developing countries.

A Tanzanian health worker holding a rural clinic.

Debt, closely linked to poverty, forces families such as this one to live on the streets of Brazil.

Debt is nothing new. It is found throughout human history and in every society. Many people know what it feels like to be in debt. Perhaps you have borrowed money from family or friends. In the future you may use credit cards, buy a house with a mortgage, or take out a loan for a car.

Debt can sometimes be a way of juggling financial commitments and of paying in advance for things that you really need. But it has a darker side. Imagine how you would feel if you were deeply in debt and unable to repay what you owed. The consequences for many people can be disastrous.

FACT

As the debt crisis continues, the gap between the world's richest and poorest countries is growing. The top fifth of the world's people living in the richest countries have 86 percent of the world's gross domestic product (GDP) while the bottom fifth have just 1 percent.

Personal debt

Today, people in the richer countries of the world live in a society where credit is easily available. The average American household owes more than $14,500 on top of their mortgage. Banks and credit card companies often encourage people to take out loans. They then make money by charging interest. People can find themselves with growing debts if

Automatic teller machines being used in Hong Kong, a consumer society where many people have easy access to money.

they are unable to keep up with interest payments. This may be because of a sudden life-changing event, such as a business failure, loss of employment, accident, or illness. But for many households, debt is a means of survival. Despite the relatively high standard of living in the United States as a whole, a great many people, especially working families, are deeply in debt. This is not necessarily because they are buying luxury items, but because they have had to borrow money for essentials, such as clothing, bedding, or furniture.

VIEWPOINT

"Whatever the detailed history of today's debt-ridden countries, those who could be blamed least, the poorest people in the poorest countries, have suffered most."
Cardinal Basil Hume, former Archbishop of Westminster, England

For example, when Mr. Johnson was laid off from his job and began to collect unemployment, which did not pay as much as he had been earning at work, the Johnson family found themselves having to borrow money for living expenses. With two children in school, there were always new bills on top of the basic ones. Their income was now too low to borrow from a bank. Instead they were forced to take out a much higher-interest loan from a private lender. The Johnsons soon found that despite cutting back on many essentials they were now falling behind in their credit-card payments. They were forced to take out another loan and found themselves in a downward cycle, plunging deeper and deeper into debt. Their problems were only eased with the help of a community finance project that helped them to find a way of repaying their debts with fairer, lower-interest loans until Mr. Johnson could find work again.

FACT

The world's richest countries have debts, too. In fact, the United States is the world's biggest debtor nation. In 2002 its national debt stood at about $6 trillion. This is three times the debt of all developing countries put together.

Job seekers in Japan, where unemployment and debt are growing problems.

Across the world, debt took on a different face for Kishnan, age sixteen, from India. When his father borrowed a tiny sum of money from a local landowner to pay for medical treatment for Kishnan's mother, he agreed that his son would work as a full-time servant to repay the debt. Kishnan became a bonded laborer. But since he was never paid there was no hope of clearing the debt. He was told that he would be beaten unconscious if one of the buffaloes he was herding strayed. His life was ruled by fear. With no money, education, or experience of life, it was impossible for him to escape. Eventually Kishnan was rescued by a local organization that campaigns to set bonded laborers free. Today debt bondage is a major form of slavery. It is estimated that 20 million people worldwide are trapped by it.

An adult bonded laborer at work in a quarry in India.

International debt

As you can see, ordinary people can find themselves spiralling into debt, often through no fault of their own. Many of the same principles operate for poorer countries that have borrowed from institutions and governments in richer countries. The amounts of these debts are huge. In 1999, they came to a total of $2.5 trillion. That is equal to the combined gross national product (GNP) of all the world's developing countries.

Often, when individuals or businesses fall into heavy debt, they are declared bankrupt. The slate of debt is wiped clean and they are given a fresh start. However this is not the case with countries. Debts continue even though governments and generations of citizens change.

Today the debts of the world's poorest countries are so huge that many experts question whether those countries will ever be able to repay what they owe. Worse, these debts are growing every day. Like the Radley family, governments cannot afford to keep up with the interest repayments and so the sums of money owed rise steadily. In 1980 the total amount of money that developing countries owed was $603 billion. Since then, debtor countries have repaid billions of dollars, yet they still owed more than $5 trillion in 2002.

These figures may seem so large that they are difficult to comprehend. However, as we will see in this book, debt is not just about the world of finance and economics. It is a social and moral issue, and it is about the lives of ordinary people like Alfredo and Lucy. Most of us would agree that people are the real wealth of nations. If they can develop their potential and lead productive, creative lives, their countries will benefit and develop.

VIEWPOINTS

"Should we really let our people starve so that we can pay our debts?△12 ...If African governments are really representing their people, they cannot accept conditions that would lead to more hunger, to social chaos, to civil war."
President Julius Nyerere of Tanzania

"The laws of economics ...are like the laws of engineering. There's only one set of laws and they work everywhere."
Lawrence Summers, U.S. representative on the IMF (International Monetary Fund) governing board, explaining that there is little choice over the way that debts are handled

Yet in poorer countries across the world, the burden of debt is shattering the hopes of millions. Today 1.2 billion people around the world live on less than $1 a day. They are unable to make the most of their lives or have real choices in what they do. People living in poverty lose something very precious: the chance of a long, healthy, and productive life.

Bangalore is one of the richest cities in India, yet the poor have very limited opportunities.

In this book we will be seeing how debt prolongs poverty and makes it worse. Despite good intentions, many governments cannot afford to provide their citizens with basic services such as healthcare and education. The dice are loaded against the poorest countries of the world. When they first took out loans, this seemed to be a sensible way to develop their economies and the

potential of their people. However, like the Johnson family, they then found it very difficult to break out of a downward spiral into ever-larger debts.

The enormous scourge of poverty explains why the debt crisis is seen by many as one of the most important political and moral issues of our time. The future of many countries and billions of people depend on it being resolved successfully. This book explores some of the debates that surround debt. Should countries be forced to pay debts when their people are suffering poverty? Is it fair that some countries should be helped to pay off their debts, while others are not? The next chapter examines how the debt crisis began in the first place, and why some countries have found themselves unable to repay their debts.

DEBATE

Should new leaders of countries inherit the debts of their predecessors when the money was borrowed under unfair or illegal circumstances? For example, when Nelson Mandela, former President of South Africa, was elected in 1994, he inherited more than $18 billion in debts. This was money borrowed by the apartheid state responsible for oppressing the majority of South Africans.

HOW DID THE DEBT PROBLEM START?

Just as individuals need to borrow money sometimes, so do governments. Borrowing is essential for economies to function well. Governments often need more money than they are able to raise through trade and taxes. Debt is only a problem if it cannot be repaid.

Most of today's heavily indebted countries are former colonies. These countries were taken over by Europeans or dominated by the United States, who saw them as rich sources of raw materials such as precious metals and spices. After 1898, only two African countries, Abyssinia (later Ethiopia) and Liberia remained independent. Latin America had been taken over by the Spanish and Portuguese. Meanwhile, the Europeans controlled parts of Southeast Asia in order to protect their trade routes for sugar, spices, and silks.

The legacy of colonialism

Although the colonizers talked about civilizing and educating the colonized, they did little to help the longer-term development of their colonies. They behaved in a way that simply transferred wealth to Europe. Farmers were forced to grow cash crops, such as cotton, sugar and cocoa, for export, even though this left them less land to grow their own food on. Gradually, developing countries became dependent on one or two main export commodities, and this pattern continues today. Colonialism set the stage for unequal relations between developing and industrialized countries. It also sowed the seeds of the current debt crisis.

Awash with money

Today's debt crisis began in 1973 when the world's oil-exporting countries joined together to raise the price of oil. This strategy paid off. They made huge profits and invested this oil money in commercial banks in the world's richer countries.

The banks were now eager to invest this money quickly. They offered loans, at very low interest rates, to governments in developing countries. Western governments encouraged this because they hoped that borrowers would use the money to buy goods from them. This would help to keep their economies healthy and avoid a recession.

For their part, the governments of many developing countries were eager to borrow. They wanted to keep their factories running and they needed money to pay for higher oil costs. They also looked forward to developing their economies by building roads, factories, and irrigation projects. Many governments used the money to build new hospitals and schools.

DEBATE

Between 1503 and 1660, 408,000 lbs (185,000 kg) of gold and 35,000,000 lbs (16,000,000 kg) of silver were shipped from Latin America to Europe without any payment to the indigenous people who mined the precious metals. Do the benefits gained by richer nations from their former colonies outweigh the help given to developing countries by the developed world in more recent times?

Building the Brazilian Trans-Amazon Highway, which cost over $1 billion in development loans in the 1970s.

It is true that large sums of money were spent irresponsibly by undemocratic governments. The banks were prepared to lend to any government, no matter how corrupt. They also favored large-scale projects. Often, little was done to check whether or not these projects were going to be useful. In the Philippines, for example, $2.1 billion was spent on the construction of a nuclear power plant. The project was then abandoned after it was found to be located on a dormant volcano.

Between 1970 and 1994, Zaire (now Democratic Republic of the Congo) received $8.5 billion in loans and aid. Most of this went into the personal bank accounts of President Mobutu.

Some governments, especially military rulers in Latin America, spent borrowed money on weapons. Other corrupt politicians deposited the money into their own bank accounts in the richer countries.

Crisis looms

Developing countries were advised to concentrate on exporting cash crops and raw materials. But since so many countries were given the same advice and produced the same crops, markets became flooded and prices fell. By the mid-1970s the prices of raw materials were falling.

Two other events made the situation worse. In 1979, oil prices rose again. Soon after, interest rates rose sharply. Non-oil-producing developing countries found that they were earning less, but they had to pay more for imported fuel and it cost more to borrow. They became increasingly unable to meet the costs of their debts.

The bubble bursts

In 1982, Mexico announced that it could not repay its debts. As other indebted countries considered whether they too should default, a catastrophe loomed. According to one banker, "It was like an atom bomb being dropped on the world financial system." The International Monetary Fund (IMF) and the World Bank, two of the most powerful economic organizations in the world, stepped in and began to take over the debts owed to commercial banks. Today, most debt is owed to these international organizations rather than to countries or banks.

The IMF and the World Bank had been set up toward the end of World War II, around the same time as the United Nations. At that stage there was a strong feeling that the economic downturn and unemployment that had given rise to fascism in Europe should never be allowed to occur again. These two institutions would regulate the international financial system, support the rebuilding of Europe and Japan, and bolster the development of poorer countries.

> ## FACT
> Falls in the prices paid for raw materials are closely linked to debt. Coffee prices have fallen by 70 percent since 1997. By 2002 this had cost developing countries $8 billion in lost earnings.

> ## FACT
> Poorer countries often end up with much more in debt repayments than the amount they borrowed. Costa Rica borrowed less than $6 million (£4 million) from Britain in 1973. It has paid back over $11 million (£7 million) and still owes more than $1.5 million (£1 million).

Adjusting to debt

From 1982 onward the IMF and World Bank began to play a very important role in the fortunes of developing countries.

In the 1980s, indebted countries were told that they would still have to repay their debts. To make sure that this happened, they were required to reorganize their economies and follow "structural adjustment programs."

If they did not sign up for structural adjustment programs, indebted countries would receive no further loans to import the goods they needed to keep their economies afloat. In many instances, development aid from governments was given on condition that adjustment programs were in place.

An adjustment program has several key features:
- Governments must reduce their spending, including on social services such as health and education.
- They have to export more raw materials and cash crops.
- State industries are taken over by private companies, as it is believed that this will make them more profitable.

According to its supporters, the pain of structural adjustment is justified because it will help a country's economy to grow. Eventually the benefits of growth will trickle down to the poor. However, critics say that adjustment hits the poorest people hardest. The poor have less to cushion them against its harsh effects, and even measures that try to soften the blow are temporary and do not reach everyone. There have been calls for "adjustment with a human face" that protects the most vulnerable people.

Structural adjustment advice in Ghana—but does it help?

Structural adjustment has proved very painful for people living in indebted countries. For example, Julio Cespedes and his family live in Bolivia. In 1985 the government began a structural adjustment program and it was forced to close down state factories and mines. Julio was among 20,000 miners who lost their jobs. He and his family moved to the city in search of work. There, life became harder still. Under structural adjustment, subsidies on food were cut. Prices went up but wages did not. In state schools the government no longer had any money to pay for equipment or teachers. The family could not afford the school fees now needed to educate the children. They were among the millions who saw their standard of living deteriorate under structural adjustment.

VIEWPOINT

"The economic policies imposed on debtors by the major multilateral agencies and packaged as 'structural adjustment' have cured nothing at all. They have, rather, caused untold human suffering and widespread environmental destruction."
Susan George,
British economist

THE EFFECTS OF DEBT ON EDUCATION

Angelus Mtego, aged fifteen, is in his final year at primary school in Tanzania. Children are supposed to start school here at five, but most start later. Like all his classmates, Angelus would like to go on to secondary school. However, his family is too poor to pay his primary school fees of 3,000 Tanzanian shillings (about $3.20) a year, let alone the $93 a year fees for secondary school. The biggest hurdle that Angelus faces is the cost of education.

Since he realizes that education holds the key to his future, Angelus has been paying for his own education since the age of twelve. As well as working on the family farm, he has his own quarter-acre (1,000 square-meter) plot of land. He grows beans and spends the money he makes from selling them on school fees for himself and his brother, notebooks and pens, and his school uniform.

Education will make a huge difference to the lives of these girls in Kenya.

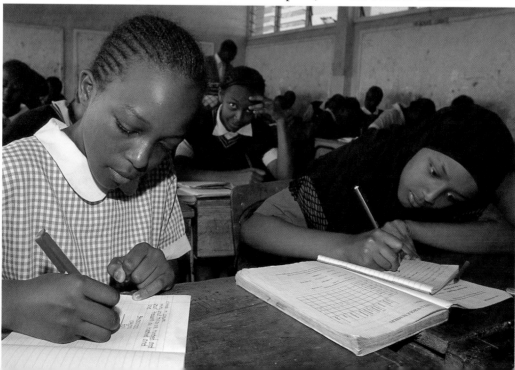

Why does education matter?

Angelus makes such efforts because he knows that an education will help him earn a better living and have more choices in his life when he is older. Imagine how different your life would be if you could not read, write, and do math. You would not be able to read timetables or instructions; you would find it difficult to apply for jobs. When you did start working you would probably be poorly paid. It would be difficult for you to read contracts or paychecks, so you might not realize if you were being cheated out of money.

An adult literacy class in Bolivia. A quarter of all adults in developing countries are illiterate.

Education is seen as being so important that the United Nations Declaration of Human Rights states that everyone has the right to a free primary education. But not everyone is able to claim this right. If you are reading this book in Europe or North America, you can expect to spend up to thirteen years at school without paying. Yet a child who lives in Mozambique will probably only go to school for two to three years.

Education for all?

Today there are still 125 million children who never go to school, roughly equal to all the six- to fourteen-year-olds in Europe and North America. On top of this, around the world 150 million children start school but drop out before they are able to read and write effectively.

Millions of children, like this boy in India, miss school because they work for a living.

Most children who miss out on schooling live in poorer countries. Within these countries, there are reasons why some children miss out more than others. For example, parents who are less well-off may not be able to afford school fees, or children may be needed to help bring in the family income. Children who live in rural areas rather than a town or city are much less likely to live near a school.

Minority groups also find that their access to education is restricted. In Mexico, for instance, indigenous people are five times more likely to be illiterate because they do not have the same

FACT

It has been estimated that each additional year of education that a girl receives will lower the child mortality rate by about 8 percent, saving 2 million lives a year.

opportunities as their peers at school. And wherever they live, girls are more likely to be kept away from school. They are usually the first to stay at home to do housework or look after younger siblings. They are also the most likely to be taken out of school if there is a crisis in the family.

Debt and education

There is no doubt that the burden of debt keeps children out of school. Primary schooling in Tanzania, where Angelus lives, used to be compulsory and free. Yet Tanzania has debts that it cannot repay. In 1993, the Tanzanian government agreed to a structural adjustment program. As part of this, it had to cut its spending on education. Teachers' salaries were reduced and education was no longer free. Class sizes grew so that there could be fifty children in a class. Can you imagine trying to learn in such crowded conditions? Schools can no longer afford to buy equipment such as desks, and school buildings have fallen into disrepair.

VIEWPOINT

"We know a great deal about who the poor are, where they are, and how they live. We understand what keeps them poor and what must be done to improve their lives."
Barber Conable, then World Bank President, speaking in 1990

There is so little equipment in their schools that these children in Mali buy their own desks and carry them home for the holidays.

In Ghana and many other countries, classes are often held outside.

In 1999, the Tanzanian government spent four times as much on debt repayments as on primary education. Yet everyone realizes that education is essential for development. Economic growth cannot happen unless people are trained and educated. In recognition of this, the government has negotiated with the IMF and abolished school fees. There are plans that all children will go to school by 2005. But it remains to be seen if this can be achieved while Tanzania has such large debts.

Studies in agriculture and industry have shown that an educated workforce adapts more easily to new technologies and so is able to produce more. In Uganda it has been found that four years of primary education will raise the amount a farmer produces by 7 percent. This makes a big difference. It means farmers can afford medicines for a sick child, can buy new tools and seeds, or pay for extra food if harvests fail.

An uncertain future

Governments around the world have agreed that providing children with education would reduce worldwide poverty and would make economic sense. To put all the world's children through primary school would cost about $9 billion a year. This one step would eradicate illiteracy within a generation. It may seem a large sum of money, yet it is less than half what Americans spend each year on toys.

VIEWPOINTS

"I have read that our country is stabilizing [following a structural adjustment program]. That may be true, but we have no jobs. We can't send our children to school. Maybe stabilizing is a good thing for the countries we pay debt to, but here life is getting harder."
Zambian woman

"Structural adjustment policies should protect appropriate funding levels for education."
World Declaration on Education for All, Jomtien, Thailand

THE EFFECTS OF DEBT ON EDUCATION

Education is such an important weapon in the fight against poverty that in 1990 representatives from 155 governments met at an international conference in Jomtien, Thailand. They promised to get rid of the problem of illiteracy and set up a plan that would give every child in the world a good primary education by the year 2000.

Ten years later, the governments of richer countries promised that "no countries seriously committed to education for all will be thwarted in their achievements of this goal by lack of resources." The target for free primary education for all has now been extended to 2015 by the World Bank. Yet despite these promises millions of children never see the inside of a classroom. Debt repayments continue to stop poorer countries from providing basic education for their people.

DEBATE

Should countries be forced to continue paying their debts if it means that they cannot afford to educate their children? Or should structural adjustment programs contain measures to make sure that education remains free?

Education goes beyond the classroom. These women in India are learning about pesticides and safety.

THE EFFECTS OF DEBT ON HEALTH

VIEWPOINTS

"My daughter is sick, but what am I supposed to do? If I take her to the clinic, I cannot afford to pay for treatment—so what is the point? If I stay at home to care for her, how will we buy the food we need to stay alive?"
Mother from Harare, Zimbabwe

"It is a debt that asks people to ask themselves: Should I buy medicine for my kids or should I pay this debt? In our case, people have to pay this debt out of poverty, so they are depriving their children of medicine or education so that they can pay off the debt. This debt did not give us any profit. But still we have to pay the debt."
Rogate Mshana, General Secretary of the Lutheran Church in Tanzania

If you live in one of the world's richer countries you can expect to live a long and reasonably healthy life. You may even take your health for granted. But for millions of people staying healthy is not so easy.

Whether they live in rich or poor countries, the poor are most likely to fall ill. They have less money to spend on wholesome food, and less land to grow it.

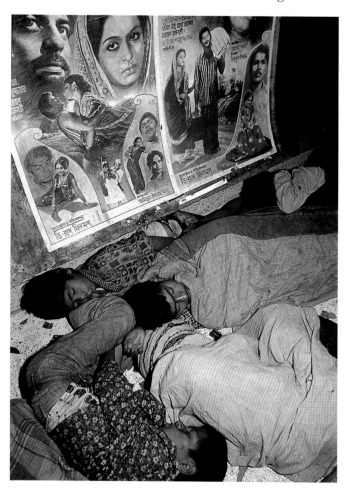

The health prospects of these street children in Calcutta, India, are poor.

They are more likely to live in areas with poor water supplies and chemical and other pollution, and they may be unable to afford medicines if they do fall sick.

Ill health can have disastrous consequences for a whole family. Even a short period of illness can push a family into crisis, as in Kishnan's story in Chapter 1. It is difficult for someone who is ill to work. If one or more family members is unable to earn a wage, the family may have to sell land or animals. This will make it even harder to make a living, and they will sink further into poverty.

Diseases of poverty

Most illnesses in developing countries could be prevented if more money were available. For this reason, they are often called "diseases of poverty." Every year 11 million children under the age of five die from preventable causes. (This means more than 30,000 deaths each day.) Diarrhea, for example, takes the lives of 4.6 million children a year. It is a simple but dangerous illness caused by dirty water. If everyone were able to drink clean water, 80 percent of sickness in the world could be avoided. Yet nearly 1 billion people do not live within easy reach of clean water.

Would you be able to stay healthy when your only source of water was next to a garbage dump?

Debt and health

It could be argued that a government's most important responsibility is to protect the lives and health of its people. Yet, since the debt crisis began, government spending on healthcare has fallen in many of the world's poorest countries.

Structural adjustment programs push poor people closer to ill health. They mean that people get lower wages because of lack of education. This, together with higher food prices, means that people become malnourished and more prone to illness. Families also have to work longer hours to make ends meet. They have less time to spend on activities that would help them to stay healthier, such as preparing food safely or obtaining clean water.

Governments of indebted countries have also had to cut back on their health spending. For example, in the mid-1970s, over 9 percent of Jamaica's budget was spent on health. By 1988, eleven years after the introduction of structural adjustment programs, this had fallen to just over 5 percent. Rural health centers are often the first to close, even though most people live in these areas. Indebted countries often find that they cannot afford to buy medicines and equipment from other countries or to pay health workers.

Immunization has saved millions of children from death and disability. But governments are finding it harder to pay for.

Passing the costs to the poor

Governments, encouraged by the IMF and the World Bank, have tried to save money by charging people for healthcare. But passing on the costs to the poor can have serious consequences. In Zimbabwe, for instance, the government aimed to increase the money it raised from charging fees from Z$15 million ($281,500) to Z$45 million ($844,500) between 1991 and 1993.

During this short time, it was found that the number of women who died while giving birth almost doubled. Most of those who died decided not to go to the hospital because they could not afford the fees. Faced with so many deaths, the government stopped charging fees in clinics in rural areas.

FACT

In 1998, Nicaragua's total health budget was $88 million. More than four times that amount was spent on debt repayments.

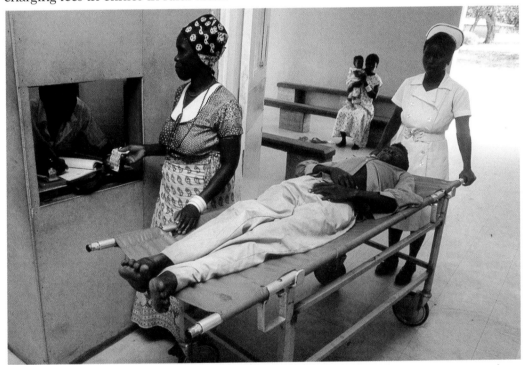

Looking at Mozambique

One country that has started to make its people's health a priority is Mozambique. From 1964 to 1992, the country was engulfed in one of the most brutal civil wars ever waged in Africa. More than a million people lost their lives. Five million people were forced to flee their homes. Half of all schools and health centers were destroyed.

This woman in Zambia has to pay before her husband can be treated in a hospital.

After peace was agreed on in 1992, Mozambique's government and people set about repairing the damage. Yet the burden of debt repayments has made this a difficult task. Today less than 40 percent of the population has access to health services.

In 2001, Mozambique qualified for some debt relief (see Chapter 8) and this has led to health spending rising by $13 million a year. However, the country is still spending more on debt than on health. To make matters worse, it is also recovering from a series of severe floods that destroyed much of the rebuilding that had already been done.

The Democratic Republic of Congo and HIV/AIDS

Debt also stops countries from dealing with some of the biggest threats to their development. HIV/AIDS is a virus and disease that has exploded dramatically in highly indebted countries. At the end of 2001, about 40 million people worldwide were living with

These children are some of the 1.7 million in Uganda who have lost one or both parents to AIDS.

HIV/AIDS. The worst-affected area was sub-Saharan Africa. Although the region is home to just 10 percent of the world's population, 70 percent of all new HIV infections in the world and more than 80 percent of AIDS deaths occurred here in 2001.

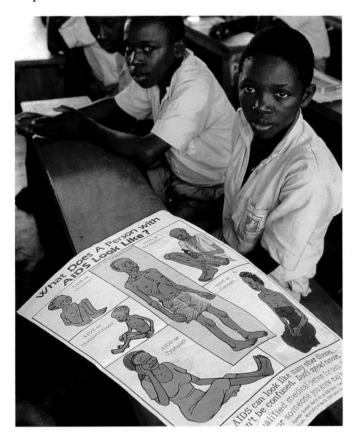

Learning about HIV/AIDS is an important way of preventing its spread.

The spread of HIV/AIDS severely hampers the economic progress of countries. It absorbs large portions of health budgets. It stops governments from meeting the needs of their people. As most victims of AIDS are young adults in the prime of their working lives, their deaths leave very young children without parents. These orphans are often left penniless because their parents had to sell everything to pay for medicines. In villages affected by HIV/AIDS, land is often left uncultivated, so there is less food available.

FACT

The average cost of treatment for AIDS in a developed country amounts to $15,000 per person per year. In Uganda, expenditure on healthcare per person is $9 per year.

Emma Tshamputu, age twenty-one, lives in the Democratic Republic of Congo and knows the havoc that HIV/AIDS can wreak. She is one of more than a million HIV/AIDS orphans in a country that has already been ravaged by war.

When she was thirteen, Emma's father died. She had to leave school and begin supporting her two younger brothers. Luckily, Emma was put in touch with a community project that gives children orphaned by AIDS life skills that will help them to earn a living. Emma learned to sew. Today she earns about $15.50 a month by making clothes. Her earnings are just enough to pay for food and

Malaria is one of the world's deadliest diseases, killing up to two million people every year. This is a children's malaria ward in Cameroon, where health services are stretched to the breaking point.

for Emma's brothers to finish their schooling. Although her childhood was taken from her by HIV/AIDS, Emma has provided a brighter future for her brothers.

AIDS thrives in sub-Saharan African countries like the Democratic Republic of Congo partly because the burden of debt stops governments from providing good healthcare. In Africa, average spending on health is just $11 per person per year. In some countries the figure is as low as $3.25. Even when services are available, people cannot afford to use them. In the poorest countries in Africa, fewer than one in five children gets a good education. Without good schooling, it is much more difficult for people to get the information and skills that help them to stay safe from HIV/AIDS. Debt also stops governments from being able to respond to the HIV/AIDS crisis. As the healthcare systems are pushed to the breaking point, increasing numbers of people are questioning the justice of debt repayments.

We are living in an age of great scientific and medical advances. Today's technological progress could lead to vaccines for malaria and HIV/AIDS. Yet most of the world's people are left out of the loop of progress, and one reason for this is debt. Since the debt crisis broke, the numbers of children who die before the age of five or before the age of one have risen in many deeply indebted countries, including Zimbabwe, Zambia, Nicaragua, Chile, and Jamaica. Diseases that were thought to have been eradicated—such as tuberculosis and yellow fever—are making a comeback in some countries as treatment and vaccination coverage declines. The health of millions of people depends on finding an end to the debt problem.

VIEWPOINT

'The health, the growth, the education and life of millions of children will be sacrificed on the altar of ...economic adjustment programs.'
UNICEF

DEBATE

In 2001, world leaders at a summit in Genoa, Italy, promised $1.2 billion to pay for the fight against AIDS. Yet how useful is this when debt repayments prevent poor countries from providing the basic health services that their people need?

THE DEBT BOOMERANG

A migrant family in Indonesia, forced by poverty to try to make a living from the rain forest.

Debt does not only affect people like Angelus, Julio, and Emma who live in developing countries. Its consequences spread much further. This chapter looks at the increasing price that is being paid by those living in the richer countries of the world. One way or another, the debt crisis affects every one of us.

Our fragile earth

Debt forces countries to use up their raw materials in the most rapidly profitable way. The world's forests are paying a heavy price for this. It is no coincidence that the countries of the world with the largest debt burdens, such as Brazil, Indonesia and Nigeria, are also those with the worst records for environmental destruction. Tropical timber is a valuable cash crop. Its export provides countries with a short-term way of paying off debts, but also creates enormous long-term problems.

For example, Indonesia is one of the most biologically rich countries in the world, even though it occupies only 1.3 percent of the land's surface. It is home to 10 percent of the world's remaining forests, where endangered species such as the

Sumatran tiger and orangutan live. As Indonesia's debts grew from $53 billion in 1989 to $151 billion in 1998, logging has been seen as a solution.

Every year, a million hectares (2.5 million acres) of forest are cut down in Indonesia. Much of this is commercial logging. However, as roads are cut through forests, poor people who have no land are able to enter them. Many of these people have seen their standard of living fall as Indonesia has suffered an economic crisis. They burn the forest to clear land and grow food, using the nutrients in the soil that are left behind in the ash. However, after a few harvests, the fertility of the ash and the soil is exhausted. So they soon find that they have to move on to a fresh plot. If this cutting down of rain forest continues at the same rate, loggers will destroy Indonesia's age-old forests in another three decades.

VIEWPOINT

"If the Amazon is the lungs of the world, then debt is its pneumonia."
Luís Lula Inácio da Silva. Brazilian trade unionist and Workers Party leader

These logs are ready to be transported to a sawmill in Indonesia.

Although you live a long way from Indonesia, what happens there directly affects you. We share one environment. And we need the world's forests because they help the earth to absorb greenhouse gases. It is now widely agreed that the changes we are seeing in the world's weather are caused at least in part by greenhouse gases.

Flooding in Great Britain in late 2000 caused a billion pounds ($1.5 million) worth of damage.

The war on drugs

As farmers in developing countries have seen the prices of their exports fall, some have been turning to another commodity that guarantees a higher income—drugs. In the richer countries of the world the drug trade is expanding rapidly. It is threatening neighborhoods with crime and violence. But for the farmers in developing countries who grow the crops, it is a lifeline. In Bolivia, for instance, the income from a hectare of coca is thirteen times more than that for corn and over three times that for cocoa. The drug trade provides small incomes for hundreds of thousands of poor peasants who would otherwise be destitute, though the big incomes are made by dealers.

Coca leaves have always been grown in Bolivia for medicinal and ritual purposes; they are far less strong than processed varieties of the drug that make cocaine. When the tin market collapsed in 1985, unemployment in Bolivia spiralled. Hundreds of thousands of people moved to the Chapare coca-growing region where a small piece of land could earn the farmer $1,200 a year. Coca became an important source of income for Bolivia and made up between 28 and 53 percent of the value of Bolivia's total exports. One in ten people in the workforce were involved in the drugs industry.

In 1989, the U.S. government declared a "war on drugs" and called for the eradication of coca crops. The move has led to widespread protests. Farmers say that they have no other way to earn a living. It is questionable whether the war on drugs is working. Production may have slowed in Bolivia and Peru, but it has skyrocketed in Colombia, where the impact of the "war on drugs" has been less dramatic.

Growing coca is the only way that this farmer in Bolivia can support his family.

DEBATE

Peru, Afghanistan, Bolivia, Burma, and Colombia are all countries that are deeply in debt. They are also among the ten countries with the highest share of fertile land being used for growing the main illegal drugs: opium, coca, and cannabis. Should richer nations bear some of the responsibility for finding alternatives to growing drugs?

It is likely that farmers who live in poverty will always be attracted to a crop that promises a steady income. For this reason, many argue that the debt crisis has to be addressed before the drug problem can be solved. If the poverty caused by debt and structural adjustment is eased, the power of the illegal drug market should be reduced.

Trade meltdown

In order to reduce their spending, indebted countries often export as much as possible and cut back on imports. The effects of this imbalance are felt in richer countries, too. Companies find that they are unable to export equipment and other manufactured goods to countries that are struggling to pay off debts. In such circumstances, employees may lose their jobs.

Before the debt crisis broke, for example, Europe sold about a fifth of its exports to the developing world, particularly Africa. By 1990 it was little more than a tenth. When the debt crisis was at its height in the 1980s, it caused the loss of about half a million jobs or potential jobs each year in the industrialized world. Over the years of the debt crisis, millions of manufacturing and agricultural jobs have been lost as markets have shrunk.

Unemployed workers in Berlin in 1998, when German unemployment rose to a record 4.546 million.

War and social unrest

Of the ten most indebted countries in the world, eight have suffered civil war or violent conflict since 1990. While it cannot be said that debt directly causes war, there are strong connections between the two. The costs of war have helped plunge many developing countries into debt in the first place. For example, during the Cold War, military governments borrowed enormous sums of money to buy weapons. One estimate suggests that between 1960 and 1987 governments in developing countries borrowed around $400 billion to fund arms imports.

Today many of the countries that were once ruled by military dictators, such as El Salvador, Uganda, and the Democratic Republic of Congo, have democratically elected governments. Yet they still find themselves paying the debts of previous governments.

An arms exhibition in London, England. Two-thirds of world arms sales are from richer countries to developing countries.

VIEWPOINT

"More dangerous than not paying the debt is for Argentines to continue dying in the streets of hunger, poverty, and marginalization."
President Fernando de la Rúa, 2001

While debt may not always lead to war, it can cause major disruption. It is difficult for governments to govern properly when people are living on welfare and cannot afford to pay taxes. The pressures that poor people face after structural adjustment have led to waves of angry demonstrations on every continent.

In 2001, Argentina, Latin America's third largest economy, was drowning in debt and faced collapse. A recession and cuts in government spending (that were part of the debt-repayment conditions) had caused widespread poverty, with a third of the population living on less than $4.64 a day. In December, tens of thousands of angry Argentineans took to the streets. Riot police fired tear gas to disperse the crowds and violence erupted. Dozens of people were killed and hundreds injured. Over the next two weeks, five presidents were to take office in Argentina. The effects of such unrest will be felt for a long time to come.

Although nine out of ten wars take place in developing countries, people in richer countries still feel their effects. One of the most obvious ways is through the need for peacekeeping missions in unstable or dangerous regions around the world. Countries around the world provide troops and equipment for United Nations peacekeeping forces. In recent years these have been sent to countries including Kosovo, East Timor, and Sierra Leone.

FACT

Since 1991, 45 percent of Argentine students have left high school because of lack of money. At the end of 2001, unemployment had reached 18.3 percent, the highest in the country's history.

Social unrest and war also force people to leave their homes. There are 22 million refugees in our world. They have left their homes because of conflict or a fear of persecution. The vast majority of refugees fled to developing countries, which struggle to provide a sanctuary despite their very limited resources.

Since the September 11, 2001 attacks on the United States, every nation has become much more aware that violence in one part of the world can spill over across the globe. We are reminded that the human misery and loss of life caused by continuing conflicts in the world is not confined to one country. In our "global village" the plight of those experiencing war and unrest affects us all. Debt is one destabilizing force in the world that could be reduced relatively easily.

These refugees at a health post in Kenya have fled from the civil war in their own country, Somalia.

IS AID THE ANSWER?

One way of improving the lives of the world's poorest people is aid. Most people think it is important to give money to charities so that they can help the poor. Perhaps you have raised money for charity yourself through a sponsored event.

It is certainly true that aid can be a valuable weapon in the fight against poverty, and there are many different types of aid that can be given. But is it really the best solution to the problem of poverty?

The idea of aid is not a new one. After World War II, the Allies decided to rebuild Europe to prevent further upheaval and to stop the spread of

Aid arrives in Greece in 1950 as part of the Marshall Plan.

communism. They drew up the Marshall Plan, which the United States agreed to fund. In 1948 the U.S. Congress spent $4 billion on aid to Europe. This helped a continent recover from the devastation of war. It also helped the United States because Europe was now able to trade and buy goods made in the United States.

Who gives aid?

Governments don't give money just to show that they care, but also to keep allies and to benefit through trade with other countries. Three-quarters of aid is given by one government to another. This "official" aid is often channeled through organizations such as the World Bank and the United Nations. Charities give far less aid than governments. Although the amount of aid that they give is very small in comparison, they can often act faster and be more flexible. They frequently fill the "gaps" that are left by governments. By working with smaller, local organizations, they can meet more specific needs quickly. For example, a particular village may need a clean water supply or the women in the village could benefit from an income-generating project.

Conditional aid

Although aid may be seen as a gift, the country that receives it (the recipient) is not usually free to decide how that money is spent. There are conditions attached to aid. Since the 1980s, foreign aid from the United States and Great Britain has been given on condition that receiving countries follow structural adjustment programs.

In the past, a large proportion of aid money has been "tied." This means that the receiving country has to buy goods (such as medical supplies or water pumps) or services (such as the expertise of consultants) from the donor country.

FACT

Since 1969, the global community has agreed to a number of aid "targets." The United Nations recommends a minimum of 0.7 percent of GNP should be given as aid from richer to poorer countries. In fact this target has never been reached. In 2000, the average was 0.2 percent, with the United States, one of the richest countries in the world, giving 0.1 percent.

VIEWPOINT

"Aid is decreasing and perhaps it does not matter, if one considers the way it is used. I don't think it is effective in terms of reaching the poor. If aid ended, life would still go on."
Hope Chigudu, a community worker from Zimbabwe

Although this bulldozer was given as aid to Burkina Faso, the mechanical parts that were needed to keep it going were not.

Tied aid helps to create jobs and develop industries in donor countries. But it does not always benefit recipients. They may be required to buy equipment, for example, that does not suit local conditions. Countries may be required to import expensive goods that could be produced more cheaply locally.

It now looks as if the argument against tied aid is being won, although it is still often conditional on certain requirements being met. At the end of 2000, Britain announced it would be phasing out tied aid completely. The governments of the world's richest countries have also agreed to end certain types of tied aid.

Aid and disasters
You will probably have seen pictures of flooding, earthquakes, or other natural disasters on your television screen. At times like this, aid is a vital way of helping people to rebuild their lives. But behind the scenes the picture is more complicated.

VIEWPOINT

"If people see governments cutting aid, at the very least they should be asking loud questions. Are you cutting it because you think the reality of world poverty is less than it was? Are you cutting it because you think governments of the Western world don't have responsibilities toward the poor?"
Michael Taylor, Director of Christian Aid

Disasters such as floods and earthquakes may be the result of natural events. But their effects are much more devastating in poorer countries than they are in the United States or Japan, for instance. It is estimated that nearly 1,300 deaths worldwide are caused every week through disasters. In 2000, the overwhelming majority of these, 86 percent, occurred in Asia.

That is because disasters tend to have less devastating effects when they strike richer countries. For instance, large parts of the United States are prone to regular flooding. Since the 1930s, dams have been built to control the flow of water. A national flood insurance scheme encourages vulnerable communities to insure their homes and belongings in case of a flood. Local governments buy land on flood plains so that fewer houses are built in these areas. All these approaches have meant that when flooding does occur, less damage is done.

Developing countries cannot afford protection. When two earthquakes hit El Salvador in early 2001, more than 1,000 people were left dead and a quarter of the population was left homeless. More than half of the country's schools were damaged. Debt has hindered the repair process.

VIEWPOINT

"We lost in 72 hours what we have taken more than 50 years to build."
Carlos Flores, President of Honduras, describing the effects of Hurricane Mitch

Unlike El Salvador, Japan could afford to rebuild after the Kobe earthquake in 1995.

Residents in Honduras look at the damage done by Hurricane Mitch in 1998.

Because they live in a poorer country, people in El Salvador were harder hit when disaster struck. Most of those who were affected were the poor, who had moved nearer the capital in search of work. They had little choice over where they lived and were forced to move onto land that no one else wanted. This land was on steep, crowded hillsides that collapsed in the earthquake and buried victims in landslides. People living in poverty have fewer choices and they cannot afford insurance. They lose everything when disasters happen.

The burden of debt makes developing countries poorer and people more vulnerable. Debt stopped El Salvador from investing in the preventive measures that richer countries can afford. For example, the government could not provide housing built to withstand earthquakes. Emergency services are underfunded. The roads that could bring help to damaged areas are badly maintained.

IS AID THE ANSWER?

When disaster struck, thousands of villages were cut off for days. People did not have equipment to dig survivors from the rubble.

The vicious circle

Throughout the 1990s, Western nations were giving about $50 billion each year in aid. This may seem a large amount, but the world's poorest countries pay the West nine times more in debt repayments than they receive in aid. In 1999, interest payments to banks in the developed world amounted to $135 billion.

In this chapter we have seen how aid can be very important when it allows people to find a way out of poverty or recover from a disaster. But, as debts owed by developing countries continue to mount, more people are questioning whether aid is really the best solution to the problem of poverty.

A variety of different suggestions have been proposed. Most would agree that a first step is ending some of the disadvantages faced by poorer countries. In the next chapter we will be looking at how fairer patterns of trade can give poor people the chance to take control of their own lives.

DEBATE

In 1998, 15,000 people died and a million were made homeless when Hurricane Mitch swept through Honduras, the second poorest country in the Western hemisphere. Mitch plunged millions of people into deepening poverty. It also rekindled a global debate: Should poor nations affected by natural disasters still be forced to pay their debts?

Aid at its best. These women in Bangladesh are being lent a small sum of money to set up their own businesses.

DEBT
AND TRADE

If you think about your day so far, you will find that you have been connected to people from countries around the globe. Think about where the food you have eaten comes from. Where was the cotton that some of your clothes are made from grown? Which countries were your household goods made in? Where was this book printed? Trade is our closest link with people in other countries.

Today's patterns of world trade have been built up over centuries. We have already seen how dependent developing countries are on raw

These workers in Indonesia have been picking coffee beans. Twenty million households in the world depend on this one crop for a living.

materials; these make up three-quarters of Africa's export earnings, for example. But poorer nations do not always reap the benefits of their rich natural resources. We can see this by looking at a simple bar of chocolate.

The chocolate chain

Americans consume on average of more then 10 pounds of chocolate per person every year. Nine-tenths of the cocoa beans to make this chocolate is imported from West African countries like Ghana and the Côte d'Ivoire. But very little of the money that Europeans spend on chocolate will go to cocoa-producing countries and the 11 million Africans who depend on cocoa for their living. For example, out of a one-dollar bar of chocolate bought in the United States, only about 8 cents goes to the cocoa farmer. The rest will go to manufacturers, shippers, retailers, and federal and state governments as tax.

Debt and trade: the links

The experience of Lefkata Jere who lives in Zambia shows the links between trade and debt. Lefkata used to work as an electrician in one of his country's state-owned industries. Earlier in his working life, Zambia was one of the most prosperous nations in Africa. Trading the copper produced in vast mines generated nearly two-thirds of the country's wealth. The money was used to invest in industries and build schools and roads.

When the price of copper fell in 1975, Zambia took out loans to cover falling prices. It was hoped that the copper price would go up again. But this never happened, and Zambia's debts spiralled.

In 1992, Zambia began a structural adjustment program. State industries were privatized. Lefkata Jere lost his job and, at age fifty-eight, had to find work breaking rocks with a hammer for $8 per week.

FACT

Between 1988 and 2001 the price of coffee fell by two-thirds. Millions of small farmers were plunged further into poverty.

The World Trade Organization

Most people probably agree that if countries are to be able to reap the benefits of trade, then trade needs to be regulated in some way. The World Trade Organization (WTO), which operates from Geneva in Switzerland, was set up in 1995 and given the job of developing a set of trading rules that all countries would follow. Most countries belong to the WTO, which has 142 members.

In theory all countries should have an equal say in how the WTO runs. But in practice richer countries have more power. Twenty-eight very poor countries, such as Gambia and Malawi, cannot afford to have any representatives in Geneva. Many more, such as Bangladesh, have only one representative to cover more than forty meetings a week, while the United States has thirteen representatives. Developing countries do not get the chance to make the deals that set the rules. And if they feel they are being treated unfairly they cannot afford to pay expensive lawyers to fight for them.

A level playing field?

According to the WTO, countries should be able to trade without restrictions. But in recent years there has been growing concern that poorer countries suffer unfair disadvantages in global trade.

For instance, in order to keep farmers in richer countries in business, they are given government help (subsidies) to grow surpluses and store them. Each year richer countries subsidize their agricultural industry by $350 billion. Every farmer in the United States receives an average subsidy of $20,000. The surpluses are then sold very cheaply in developing countries. Local farmers there, who do not receive any subsidies, cannot compete with the low prices and are driven out of business.

To take another example, India is one of the world's biggest producers of milk and is an exporter of skimmed milk powder. By owning a cow and selling milk, some of the poorer farmers used to be able to earn a reasonable living. But WTO rules required that India's trade barriers be lifted. Large quantities of highly subsidized foreign milk powder arrived and this was sold at a much lower price in stores. The subsidy on European imports was $1,100 per ton. Indian farmers, with no subsidies, have been unable to compete.

Commodities traders in London, England, compete for the best prices on raw materials from developing countries.

VIEWPOINT

"With new rules, trade could become one of the greatest solutions to global poverty."
Christian Aid

One way that governments make money through trade is by taxing imports and exports. As part of their structural adjustment, developing countries have also been forced to cut back on the taxes, or tariffs, placed on imported goods. For instance, between 1990 and 1997, India reduced these taxes from an average of 82 percent to 30 percent.

Meanwhile, tariffs in the world's richest countries have increased. These barriers to trade cost developing countries an estimated $700 billion per year—fourteen times the amount of aid that they receive.

Barriers on bananas

Banana farmers on the Windward Islands in the West Indies have felt the effects of trade barriers.

Bananas are a vital export for the Caribbean, but prices have fallen in recent years.

The banana is the world's most popular fruit. Each year they are worth almost $8 billion for producer countries and they make up almost half of all money that the Windward Islands earn from exports.

For many years the Caribbean had special trade agreements with Europe, providing a safe market for their exports. However, in 1999 the WTO ruled that the European Union should stop giving favorable treatment to banana producers from the Windward Islands. This meant that farmers running small family-sized plots would have to compete with huge American-owned plantations in Latin America. The ruling spelled disaster for the local farmers, and thousands have been forced out of business.

In the midst of this crisis, some farmers have turned to an alternative—fair trade. This trading arrangement gives producers a steady income for their crop, even if the world market prices of their commodities fall. They get a fair price for what they produce and are also helped to build a better future with support and training.

Fair trade will not solve all the problems of producers in developing countries, but it is a growing market. In 2000, it had a turnover of more than $250 million. Although it still accounts for a tiny proportion of world trade, it does give consumers the chance to make a positive choice to support the farmers whose livelihoods are threatened.

It is often argued that if poorer countries had been treated more fairly in world trade markets, their burdens of debt would not be so great. Fairer trade is clearly one part of a possible solution to the debt problem. The next chapter looks at another solution: debt relief.

VIEWPOINT

"We are told that the world has changed, that because of the WTO there must be a free market in bananas. But the market should not be so free that it can destroy people's lives."
Winston Graham, banana farmer, Windward Islands

DEBT RELIEF: CAN IT WORK?

Throughout this book, we have seen the far-reaching consequences of debt and the ways in which it is closely linked to poverty. Although it may appear on the surface to be a financial issue, it goes much further than this. That is why young people like sixteen-year-old Jovana Cruz Condor have begun to take action. She belongs to a movement of working children in Peru and makes a living selling bread. As she works, she tells people that every Peruvian child owes the equivalent of $1,200 in debt. She realizes that if children like her were not forced by poverty to work, they would have more choice and control over their lives. Jovana has collected thousands of signatures calling for Peru's debt to be canceled.

One of Peru's working children cleans a car windshield in Lima.

Jubilee 2000

In the 1990s, there were growing calls for an end to the debt problem. The Jubilee 2000 movement had a big impact on public awareness of the issue. It began in 1996 in Britain and soon had members across more than sixty countries including the United States. Jubilee 2000 campaigners called for a cancellation of debt for the poorest countries in the world.

An antidebt demonstration in South Africa.

They argued that, as a new millennium approached, developing countries should be given a fresh start: The debt of fifty-one poor countries (totalling $269 billion) should be canceled by the end of 2000.

This idea of debt relief went back a long way. It was based on the Jubilee Law, enshrined in ancient Israel and described in the book of Leviticus in the Old Testament. Every fifty years slaves were to be set free, wealth was to be given back to the poor, and debts were to be canceled.

Although the Jubilee 2000 campaign led to a shift in public opinion about debt, there were those who argued against debt relief, claiming that many developing countries were badly run and corrupt. Canceling their debts would only encourage those governments to continue spending irresponsibly. Furthermore, they said that granting debt relief to all the poorest countries could undermine the whole financial system, which depends on debtors continuing to pay back loans.

DEBATE

Some lending countries claim that letting some developing countries out of their debts would be a "moral hazard." It would encourage other developing countries to be reckless. Bankers warn that forgiveness for some countries would weaken the whole structure of global finance. Should some countries have their debts "forgiven" and on what conditions?

Debt relief begins

In 1996, for the first time ever, the World Bank and the IMF agreed to reduce the debt burden of some of the poorest nations. A group of forty-two countries, mainly in Africa, were identified as Heavily Indebted Poor Countries (HIPCs). They had seen their debts more than triple since 1980 and there was little hope of escape. On average, they owed more than twice what they earned each year from exports.

Almost one in five children in HIPCs die each year before their fifth birthday, most of them from diseases related to poverty. Life expectancy averages fifty-one (twenty-six years less than that of people living in an industrialized country). Only six out of ten adults are able to read and write.

The HIPC initiative, as it was called, marked an important change in the way the debt problem was dealt with by the IMF and the World Bank. But some of the world's then most powerful countries—Germany, Italy, and Japan—opposed the initiative. There were questions over how much debt relief would cost and how the costs would be shared among the lenders.

Three years later, after strong pressure from campaigners and public opinion, world leaders met in Cologne, Germany, and the HIPC initiative was improved. The poorest countries would be able to get debt relief more quickly and would receive greater assistance, though still with conditions attached.

What does the HIPC initiative do?

To qualify for debt relief at all, countries must be "very poor," must have "unsustainable" debt burdens, and must pursue "good policies." Under the enhanced HIPC initiative, they qualify for debt relief in two stages. Firstly they need to show, over two to three years, that they are following structural adjustment programs. They also need to show that the money they save from debt relief will be used to benefit the poor.

At the end of this first stage, HIPC countries receive some debt relief on their repayments. But their overall levels of debt are not reduced or canceled. In the second stage, countries are supposed to put into action plans to reduce poverty that have been agreed on by the IMF. Their progress is monitored and, if they are successful, some of their debts are canceled.

James Wolfensohn, President of the World Bank, meets Jubilee 2000 representatives.

Is the HIPC initiative enough?

The HIPC initiative has been widely welcomed. But critics say that the conditions of debt relief are too strict and there are too many time delays in the program. By December 2001, twenty-five countries were receiving some debt relief but only four of the forty-two countries—Uganda, Bolivia, Mozambique, and Tanzania—had gone through all the HIPC stages and been given the relief promised at Cologne in 1999.

A young Haitian boy scratches a living by picking through the garbage dump.

The HIPC initiative also covers only a very small portion of the overall debt of developing countries. The IMF has estimated that the cost of the HIPC initiative would be about $28.6 billion. In 2000, the total debt of all "low income" countries was close to $600 billion.

Some of the HIPC countries are unlikely to be able to meet the conditions required and so will not qualify for any relief. There are also many more countries heavily burdened by debt. Eighty-eight countries are classified as severely indebted. One of these, Haiti, is one of the poorest countries in the world. Almost half its population is unable to read and write, but it does not qualify for debt relief because it has not met the requirements of the IMF.

It is important to remember that the HIPC initiative is not intended to end countries' debts. Its purpose is to organize them in a way that countries can afford to pay. However, since the debate on debt has gained public attention, another question has been asked: Should the debts be canceled altogether?

Debt cancellation

Some governments in richer countries have taken a lead by agreeing to cancel the debts that are owed to them. For example, in 2000, the British government announced that it would cancel all debts on condition that the money saved by the debtor countries would be spent on services to reduce poverty. This was an important gesture, but did not amount to large sums of money. The HIPC countries owed Britain a total of £2 billion ($3 billion) out of a total debt of £132 billion ($204 billion). Nevertheless, this step did put pressure on other governments to cancel their debts. If all of them did this, more than a fifth of developing countries' total debt would be canceled.

VIEWPOINT

"We must recognize that we are living with a time-bomb and, unless we take action now, it could explode in our children's faces."
James Wolfensohn, President of the World Bank, talking about easing the debt problems of the world's poor

VIEWPOINT

"As long as there is poverty in the world I can never be rich, even if I have a billion dollars... I can never be what I ought to be until you are what you ought to be. This is the way our world is made."

Martin Luther King, Junior, African-American civil rights leader

Solving the debt crisis will mean that children like this schoolgirl from India can achieve their potential.

Looking to the future

The debate over whether debt should be eased or canceled is likely to continue. The IMF and World Bank argue that there is a limited pool of money. If more and faster debt relief is provided to some countries, other ones will miss out. Others say that debt relief could easily be financed by changing the way that the IMF operates and selling some gold stocks.

In the end the question of debt relief is a moral one. The main victims of debt are the world's poorest people. In most instances they gained little from the lending that came before the debt crisis broke. Yet they now have to pay the greatest price. The United Nations has estimated that seven million children's lives could be saved each year if the debts of poor countries were canceled. At the same time, steps could be taken to ensure that development programs benefit the poor most.

As we look to the future, there are difficult questions to be answered. For example, how can trade be improved so that it contributes more to the well-being of countries and the people who live there? How can the best use be made of aid? It is also important to remember that the debt problem is not the only one facing the poorest countries of the world. Poverty existed before the debt crisis, and ending debt will not bring immediate prosperity.

We can be certain that lifting the debt burden must be a part of any solution to poverty. It is a barrier that prevents countries from

Overcoming the debt crisis will also secure a better future for these children who live in the city of Davao, in the Philippines.

providing a decent standard of living for all their people. As they continue repaying their debts, the total amount that they owe keeps growing.

The debt crisis has been compared to a time bomb. Unless a solution is found, the damage of debt and poverty will increasingly affect us all, whether we live in rich or poor countries. The future security of our shared world depends on finding a way to change the situation for the better.

DEBATE

The richest countries dominate the IMF governing body, yet they represent only 15 percent of the world's population. Should developing countries be given a bigger say in world economic affairs? How could this be achieved?

GLOSSARY

aid money, grants, and other help given by one country to another. There are several forms of aid. "Official" aid is given by governments and organizations such as the World Bank or the United Nations. "Unofficial" aid is given by charities or nongovernmental organizations (NGOs).

bonded labor a system in which people are forced to work to pay off a debt to someone who lent them money, such as a landlord.

cash crops crops that are grown to be sold for money and exported, not to be used by the people who have grown them.

Cold War a situation that existed between 1945 and the late 1980s between Western Europe and the United States on the one hand and the Soviet Union and Eastern Europe on the other. Although not actually "at war," the two sides had extremely hostile relations.

colonialism the policy and practice of a country or people extending control over other peoples or areas. Historically colonies had no real independence. They were used by the colonial powers to gain access to raw materials and markets for exports.

colony a country or people that is taken over or controlled by another country.

commercial bank a bank that is privately owned and operates to make a profit.

commodity a cash crop, or raw material, that is traded.

credit an amount of money that is lent to a person or organization on condition that it will be repaid later.

debtor an individual or nation that owes a debt.

debt relief a system by which an individual or nation is assisted with debt repayments.

debt repayment the amount of money that must be repaid on a loan.

default if countries stop debt repayment they are said to default on their loans.

developed country richer, industrialized countries are usually referred to in this book as "developed countries" and sometimes as "the West." Within developing countries there are groups of wealthy people, just as there are pockets of poverty and under-development in the richest countries.

developing country in this book, the term "developing countries" has been used to refer to the low- and middle-income countries of Africa, Asia, the Caribbean, Central and South America, and the Pacific. These countries are also sometimes called "the Third World." Many of these countries are largely dependent on agriculture, and have fewer industries.

donor a country or individual that gives aid to another. The person or country that receives the aid is called the recipient.

economy the way a country uses its resources, such as its land, people, and minerals, to produce wealth. When we look at an economy we consider how the wealth is shared and how it is traded with other countries.

exports the products a country sells to other countries.

fair trade a world market practice ensuring that producers are paid a fair (and often guaranteed) price for their produce. Coffee, tea, bananas, and chocolate are among the fair trade products available in many supermarkets.

fascism an extreme right-wing political movement that aims to unite a country's people under an all-powerful leader.

greenhouse gases gases produced mainly by activities such as burning fossil fuels (coal, oil, etc.) that contribute to heating up the global temperature and changing the world's climate.

Gross Domestic Product (GDP) the total value of goods and services in a country, without taking into account imports and exports.

Gross National Product (GNP) the total value of goods and services in a country, including imports and exports. It is commonly used to measure the wealth of a country.

HIPC initiative a program of debt relief for Heavily Indebted Poor Countries (HIPCs) launched in 1996 by the IMF and World Bank.

imports the products a country buys from other countries.

indigenous peoples the first, or original, peoples to live in an area.

insurance an agreement to compensate someone for a loss or damage in return for paying some money in advance. For example, if someone is insured against flood damage, they receive money to repair or rebuild their home in the event of disaster.

interest when people or countries lend money they expect to get back more than they lend. The extra is called interest. It can be seen as the price that is paid for borrowing.

International Monetary Fund (IMF) a global financial organization set up in 1945 to stabilize world trade and lend money to countries that needed it. The IMF often insists that countries adopt certain economic policies as a condition of being given a loan.

mortality rate the rate of death (per thousand) in a particular population.

national debt the money that all governments borrow to finance the running of the state and fund services such as healthcare, education, etc.

nongovernmental organization (NGO) a charity or voluntary organization that gives advice, money, or other help, aimed at making poorer people better off.

Organization for Economic Co-operation and Development (OECD) an intergovernmental organization of industrialized countries.

raw materials materials that are used to make something else. Timber, oil, and minerals such as coal or gold are all raw materials.

recession a period when things are not going well in an economy. Companies often produce less, and this means that unemployment rises.

structural adjustment program (SAP) a package of economic reforms that countries agree to as a condition for receiving new loans, mostly from the IMF.

subsidy money given by the state, or a public body, to reduce the prices of certain goods or services. For example, farmers are paid subsidies for crops that they grow so that market prices can be kept low, but they still receive an income.

tied aid aid that is given with "strings attached." The donor countries say that the money has to be spent on certain products or services.

United Nations (UN) an organization set up in 1945 to promote peace and co-operation among countries.

vaccination injecting a person with a mild form of a germ or virus in order to give them immunity to that disease.

World Bank an organization set up in 1944 to lend money to countries to pay for development projects.

World Trade Organization (WTO) an international body set up in 1995 to promote free and fair trade.

BOOKS TO READ

Dent, Martin and Bill Peters. **The Crisis of Poverty and Debt in the Third World.** Ashgate, 1999.

Egendorf, Laura. **Poverty.** Farmington Hills, Mich.: Gale Group, 1998.

Garlake, Teresa. **Twentieth Century Issues: Poverty.** London: Hodder Wayland, 1999.

Garlake, Teresa. **Poverty: Changing Attitudes 1900–2000.** Austin: Raintree, 1999.

Potter, George Ann. **Deeper than Debt: Economic Globalisation and the Poor.** London: Latin America Bureau, 2000.

INDEX

Numbers in **bold** refer to illustrations.